BASEBALL LEGENDS

Hank Aaron
Grover Cleveland Alexander
Ernie Banks
Johnny Bench
Yogi Berra
Roy Campanella
Roberto Clemente
Ty Cobb
Dizzy Dean
Joe DiMaggio
Bob Feller
Jimmie Foxx
Lou Gehrig
Bob Gibson
Rogers Hornsby
Reggie Jackson
Shoeless Joe Jackson
Walter Johnson
Sandy Koufax
Mickey Mantle
Christy Mathewson
Willie Mays
Stan Musial
Satchel Paige
Brooks Robinson
Frank Robinson
Jackie Robinson
Pete Rose
Babe Ruth
Nolan Ryan
Mike Schmidt
Tom Seaver
Duke Snider
Warren Spahn
Willie Stargell
Casey Stengel
Honus Wagner
Ted Williams
Carl Yastrzemski
Cy Young

NEWFIELD
PUBLICATIONS

BASEBALL LEGENDS

PETE ROSE

Thomas W. Gilbert

Introduction by
Jim Murray

Senior Consultant
Earl Weaver

CHELSEA HOUSE PUBLISHERS
New York • Philadelphia

Published by arrangement
with Chelsea House Publishers.
Newfield Publications and design
are federally registered trademarks
of Newfield Publications, Inc.

CHELSEA HOUSE PUBLISHERS
Editorial Director: Richard Rennert
Executive Managing Editor: Karyn Gullen Browne
Copy Chief: Robin James
Picture Editor: Adrian G. Allen
Art Director: Robert Mitchell
Manufacturing Director: Gerald Levine
Assistant Art Director: Joan Ferrigno
Baseball Legends
Senior Editor: Philip Koslow
Staff for PETE ROSE
Editorial Assistant: Scott Briggs
Designer: Cambraia Magalhes
Picture Researcher: Alan Gottlieb
Cover Illustration: Daniel O'Leary
Copyright © 1995 by Chelsea House Publishers, a division
of Main Line Book Co. All rights reserved.
Printed and bound in the United States of America.

Library of Congress Cataloging-in-Publication Data
Gilbert, Thomas W.
    Pete Rose / Thomas W. Gilbert; introd. by Jim Murray; senior
consultant, Earl Weaver.
        p. cm.—(Baseball legends)
    Includes bibliographical references (p.) and index.
    ISBN 0-7910-2171-8.
    1. Rose, Pete, 1941–   —Juvenile literature. 2. Baseball
players—Biography—Juvenile literature. [1. Rose, Pete, 1941–
2.Baseball players.]   I. Weaver, Earl, 1930– II. Title. III.
Series.
    GV865.R65G45 1995   94-30941
    796.357'092—dc20   CIP
        [B]   AC

CONTENTS

WHAT MAKES A STAR

Jim Murray

No one has ever been able to explain to me the mysterious alchemy that makes one man a .350 hitter and another player, more or less identical in physical makeup, hard put to hit .200. You look at an Al Kaline, who played with the Detroit Tigers from 1953 to 1974. He was pale, stringy, almost poetic-looking. He always seemed to be struggling against a bad case of mononucleosis. But with a bat in his hands, he was King Kong. During his career, he hit 399 home runs, rapped out 3,007 hits, and compiled a .297 batting average.

Form isn't the reason. The first time anybody saw Roberto Clemente step into the batter's box for the Pittsburgh Pirates, the best guess was that Clemente would be back in Double A ball in a week. He had one foot in the bucket and held his bat at an awkward angle—he looked as though he couldn't hit an outside pitch. A lot of other ballplayers may have had a better-looking stance. Yet they never led the National League in hitting in four different years, the way Clemente did.

Not every ballplayer is born with the ability to hit a curveball. Nor is exceptional hand-eye coordination the key to heavy hitting. Big-league locker rooms are filled with players who have all the attributes, save one: discipline. Every baseball man can tell you a story about a pitcher who throws a ball faster than anyone has ever seen but who has no control on or *off* the field.

The Hall of Fame is full of people who transformed themselves into great ballplayers by working at the sport, by studying the game, and making sacrifices. They're overachievers—and winners. If you want to find them, just watch the World Series. Or simply read about New York Yankee great Lou Gehrig; Ted Williams, "the Splendid Splinter" of the Boston Red Sox; or the Dodgers' strikeout king Sandy Koufax.

A pitcher *should* be able to win a lot of ballgames with a 98-miles-per-hour fastball. But what about the pitcher who wins 20 games a year with a fastball so slow that you can catch it with your teeth? Bob Feller of the Cleveland Indians got into the Hall of Fame with a blazing fastball that glowed in the dark. National League star Grover Cleveland Alexander got there with a pitch that took considerably longer to reach the plate; but when it did arrive, the pitch was exactly where Alexander wanted it to be— and the last place the batter expected it to be.

There are probably more players with exceptional ability who didn't make it to the major leagues than there are who did. A number of great hitters, bored with fielding practice, had to be dropped from their team because their home-run production didn't make up for their lapses in the field. And then there are players like Brooks Robinson of the Baltimore Orioles, who made himself into a human vacuum cleaner at third base because he knew that working hard to become an expert fielder would win him a job in the big leagues.

A star is not something that flashes through the sky. That's a comet. Or a meteor. A star is something you can steer ships by. It stays in place and gives off a steady glow; it is fixed, permanent. A star works at being a star.

And that's how you tell a star in baseball. He shows up night after night and takes pride in how brightly he shines. He's Willie Mays running so hard his hat keeps falling off; Ty Cobb sliding to stretch a single into a double; Lou Gehrig, after being fooled in his first two at-bats, belting the next pitch off the light tower because he's taken the time to study the pitcher. Stars never take themselves for granted. That's why they're stars.

4,192

On September 11, 1985, a sellout crowd of more than 47,000 people packed Cincinnati's Riverfront Stadium to see the Reds play a night game against the San Diego Padres. The Reds were in second place in the Western Division of the National League. It was a warm evening, perfect weather for baseball.

But that was not why most of the fans were there. They had come out that night to see their hometown hero Pete Rose break one of the greatest baseball records ever—the all-time mark for most career hits. The record, 4,191 hits, was set by Detroit Tigers star Ty Cobb back in 1928. It had stood unbroken for nearly 60 years.

Baseball is a game of records and numbers. Some records, like the record for most saves by a relief pitcher, seem to be broken every few years. Others are challenged so rarely that they seem almost unreal. In this category are Cy Young's 511 pitching wins, Joe DiMaggio's 56-game hitting streak, and Hank Aaron's 755 lifetime home runs. Ty Cobb's 4,191 hits once ranked near the

Pete Rose drives a single to left-center field on September 11, 1985, at Cincinnati's Riverfront Stadium. The hit was the 4,192nd of Rose's major league career, vaulting him into first place on baseball's all-time hit list.

top of this list. In order to reach that total, Cobb had batted .367—the highest career average in major league history—over 24 years. The Hall of Fame is filled with great hitters who enjoyed long careers but never got close to Cobb. Hank Aaron ended with 3,771 hits, Stan Musial with 3,630, Babe Ruth with 2,873.

As Rose stepped into the batter's box in the bottom of the first inning, the Reds fans—many

Ty Cobb, rated by many as baseball's greatest all-around player, retired in 1928 with 4,191 base hits. Most baseball fans were convinced that no one would ever surpass Cobb's astonishing total, until Rose eclipsed the mark in 1985.

of them Rose's friends and neighbors—stood and roared. They had watched and listened to the Reds game in Chicago the previous Sunday, when Rose got two hits to tie Cobb's record. They had prayed for something to stop Rose that day so that he could come back and break the record in front of the hometown fans in Cincinnati. Their prayers were answered by hard-throwing Cubs reliever Lee Smith, who struck Rose out with the game tied in the ninth inning, and by a violent thunderstorm that washed out the rest of the game. Now they stomped their feet, yelling for Rose to get the record-breaking hit.

As Riverfront Stadium continued to rock, Padres right-hander Eric Show took a little extra time staring in to his catcher for the sign. His first pitch was a high fastball for ball one. Rose set one foot outside the batter's box, pulled nervously at his batting gloves, tapped the top of his helmet, and returned to his hitting crouch. He fouled off the next pitch and took another, low, for ball two.

Show's 2-1 pitch was a slider, down and in to the left-hand-hitting Rose. As he had done so many times before, Rose drew in his hands, flicked his gleaming black bat, and inside-outed a soft liner to left-center. For a split second, it seemed that left fielder Carmelo Martinez might try for a shoestring catch, but he pulled up and played the ball on a bounce.

The crowd broke out in deafening cheers. Fireworks exploded in the night sky. Rose's teammates and a few of the Padres came out to shake his hand while the grounds crew removed first base as a souvenir. As Eric Show sat on the mound in disgust, the baseball was retrieved

Rose embraces his son, Pete junior, after stroking his record-breaking hit. The achievement was especially meaningful for Rose because it took place in his hometown, with his family, his closest friends, and thousands of longtime fans in attendance.

to be sent to the Baseball Hall of Fame in Cooperstown, New York. Reds owner Marge Schott kissed Rose and presented him with a red Corvette that had suddenly appeared on the Riverfront Astroturf. As if anyone in the ballpark could have forgotten the number, Riverfront's huge DiamondVision screen read "4,192." Pete Rose was now major league baseball's all-time hit leader.

The celebration continued. Rose's son, Pete junior, who was the Reds batboy, came onto the field and hugged his father. Pete Rose always seemed like the type of man who was incapable of crying; but at that moment both father and son were in tears. Asked later how he felt when he rounded first base after the big hit, Rose spoke of Ty Cobb and of his own late father: "I look up. I'm not a very religious person, but I see clear in the sky, my dad, Harry Francis Rose, and Ty Cobb . . . with Dad in the sky and Petey in my arms, you had three generations of Rose men together, in spite of time, in spite of change, in spite of death. So that's what it was that made me cry."

2

"PETE ROSE'S BOY"

Pete Rose (back row, fourth from left) poses with other members of the Knot-Hole Club team. Though small for his age, Pete had already developed the hustling, line drive–hitting style that would distinguish his baseball career.

Peter Edward Rose was born on April 14, 1941, in Cincinnati, Ohio. He grew up on the west side of the city, in a neighborhood called Anderson Ferry, part of the Sedamsville section along the banks of the Ohio River. The ferry that gave the neighborhood its name had begun to cross the river, back and forth between Cincinnati and Constance, Kentucky, way back in the 1830s. When Rose was born, the ferry was still operating.

The families of young Pete's playmates were working class, and most of their fathers were employed in the factories of downtown Cincinnati. But Anderson Ferry itself was a fairly rural place during Pete's childhood in the 1940s. He and his friends lived more like Huckleberry Finn and Tom Sawyer than city kids. They passed the summer afternoons climbing the muddy cliffs of the riverbank, stealing watermelons from a nearby farm, and camping overnight in the woods. When they got older, the children of Anderson Ferry played more dangerous games, like hopping rides on the freight trains that rolled alongside the river or swimming the treacherous currents of the Ohio all the way to the Kentucky side.

But the number one pastime—for children and adults alike—was sports. The life of the community revolved around a local athletic club that sponsored football, basketball, baseball, and softball teams. Years later, when someone asked Rose why he had spent so much of his boyhood playing sports, he replied, "Because there was nothing else to do."

This was particularly true for the son of Harry Francis Rose and LaVerne Bloebaum Rose. Both parents were athletic. Many people think that Pete inherited his personality from his mother, specifically her high energy level, blunt way of speaking, and elbows-out cockiness. LaVerne Rose once said of herself, "I didn't take nothing from nobody. I wouldn't stand back from a fight." Well known as a softball player before her marriage, she may also have been responsible for her son's great hitting ability. According to one neighbor, "She could really wallop the ball."

In contrast to his wife, Harry Rose was a reserved man who never had much to say. His quiet dignity commanded a lot of respect in Anderson Ferry. One of the few men in the neighborhood who wore a suit and tie to work, Harry Rose, who was nicknamed Pete, worked as a cashier for a downtown bank. He was also a splendid amateur athlete, known for his hustle and fearlessness more than his raw talent. Barely five feet nine and slightly built, he threw himself into contact sports with abandon. He boxed as a young man and played football into his forties. Pete later recalled watching one game in which his father "was blocked so hard that his hip was broken, but he managed to tackle the opposing ball carrier. He gave every-thing he had. That may be why I try to do the same." Pete idolized his father. "I get all my determination, all my habits, from my father," he later said. "He worked at Fifth-Third Bank in Cincinnati for about 38 years. . . . Before he went home the job was done. Never would take a day off. He'd go in even if he didn't feel well. . . . It's not always 'just do the big things' and don't do the little things because most of the time, if you do the little things they'll make you win. To be honest, I don't play baseball any differently than my father approached being a banker."

Possibly because he knew from experience how tough it was for a little man in a big man's game like football, Harry Rose encouraged his son to go into baseball. "His dad started him out when he was two years old," LaVerne Rose recalled. "He could hardly throw a ball. During the Summer I'd never have to worry about where he was. It has always been baseball. He'd walk three miles to find a baseball diamond if he had to." Soon, Pete's life revolved around the Knot-Hole Club, a youth league that ran baseball leagues in nearby Bold Face Park. Using the same swing that later produced 4,256 major league hits, Pete banged out line drive after line drive in Bold Face Park. Playing ball was fun, but Harry Rose and his son took it a little more seriously than most of the other fathers and sons. As Pete said later, "We like having fun in the Rose family. But is losing fun? I don't think that it is."

By the time Pete was nine years old, his father retired from playing sports himself and

A view of Sedamsville, Ohio, where Pete Rose played organized baseball for the first time. Under the guidance of his father and his uncle, young Pete learned to switch-hit and to play catcher—these talents increased his chances of eventually becoming a major leaguer.

concentrated on preparing his son for a career as a professional athlete. He was joined by his brother-in-law, Buddy Bloebaum. A former minor league baseball player and a "bird dog," or unsalaried scout, for the Reds, Bloebaum could teach Pete some of the finer points of the game. The first thing that Pete's father and uncle decided was that speed, hustle, and line drives would carry the youngster only so far. He was small for his age and gave little indication that he would grow into a major league home run hitter. In order to give him an edge, the two men taught Pete how to switch-hit and how to play catcher, the most important defensive position in baseball.

Both of Pete's teachers had dreamed of becoming professional athletes. Neither one had made it. Now they hoped to recapture their dreams through Pete.

3

"RIVER RAT"

Most future professional baseball players start out as stars. As young boys, they are usually the best players in their neighborhood or in their county. When they are a little older, they become the kind of phenoms who pitch every other game, bat cleanup, and hit .800 on their Little League teams. Pete Rose was no different.

For most young players, however, the time comes—in junior high school, in high school, or in the low minors, if they are given a professional contract—when they experience failure for the first time. How they handle that first taste of adversity often determines whether they will make it to the major leagues or not. A few become stronger; many more lose confidence and give up.

For Pete Rose, that moment came in 10th grade when he was cut by the football team at Cincinnati's Western Hills High School. At 130 pounds, Pete was too small even to be given a tryout, in the opinion of the varsity football coach. For most youngsters this would have been no big deal. After all, Pete was still on the

An aerial view of Cincinnati's Western Hills High School, which Pete Rose attended during the late 1950s. Though he excelled at basketball and baseball, young Pete also aspired to football stardom; he was devastated when the varsity football coach refused to give him a tryout.

basketball and baseball teams. But it was devastating for the son of Harry Rose, the famous all-around amateur athlete. Going back to the days when he served as the water boy for his father's football team, Pete had always walked in his father's footsteps. "Now I was cut," he later remembered, "Me. Pete Rose. Mr. Pete Rose's kid, and the coach thought I wasn't good enough to look at."

Unable to handle the disappointment, Pete started skipping classes and hanging around the streets with a crowd of tough kids who, like him, came from the poorer neighborhoods along the Ohio River. According to one high school friend, "Pete was a so-called river rat, and those types were looked down on by the rest of the school. That was his whole persona. He saw himself as a punk, or a greaser as it was called then."

Dressed in white T-shirts and tight blue jeans, the river rats looked and acted tough, but it was mostly an act. Neither Pete Rose nor his friends got into any serious trouble. The worst thing Pete did was to cut so many classes that he failed 10th grade. Today, he is still embarrassed by the way he behaved that year. "I'll tell this to every person who listens," he said recently. "There is nothing more important for a young person than getting educated. One thing in my life, if I could do differently, I would have concentrated more on getting educated." When the city of Cincinnati honored Rose by naming a downtown street Pete Rose Way, Rose joked, "They should have named an alley after me the way I acted in high school."

Rose came out of this youthful crisis with an even fiercer determination to make it in sports.

And he never entirely lost that street-smart, river-rat attitude. Even when he was a wealthy big league baseball star, driving a Porsche and living in a large suburban house, Rose still liked to see himself as an underdog, a kid from the wrong side of the tracks who had to push a little harder than everyone else to succeed.

Ineligible to play high school sports in his senior year because he had repeated the 10th grade, Pete played second base—he had never mastered catching—for Lebanon, Ohio, in the Daytona Amateur League. In this highly competitive league, Rose batted .500 and first drew the attention of scouts from major league clubs. It looked for a while as though he might sign

Rose (back row, third from right) poses with other Western Hills varsity lettermen in 1960. Despite his success as an athlete, Rose later regretted his failure to work hard in the classroom. "There is nothing more important for a young person than getting educated," he asserted.

with the Baltimore Orioles, but all that changed when his uncle Buddy Bloebaum talked Cincinnati Reds farm director Phil Seghi into offering Rose a contract for $7,000, plus an extra $5,000 if he ever lasted 30 days on the major league roster. Harry Rose wanted to give the Orioles a chance to make a counteroffer, but Pete was so happy to get a chance to play for his hometown team that he could not have cared less about the money. Two days later, 19-year-old Pete Rose reported to Geneva, New York, in the Class D New York–Penn League. He was now a professional baseball player.

Geneva was the lowest rung on the Reds minor league ladder, but it was a big step up for Rose. The level of competition was much higher than what he was used to, and the pace of professional baseball was punishing. Instead of playing a leisurely 20- or 30-game high school or amateur season and going home each night to his mother, in his first season with Geneva, Rose slept in a lonely rented room, made grueling bus trips across upstate New York and Pennsylvania, and played 85 baseball games in three months.

Not surprisingly, Rose's debut in pro ball was a disappointment. He hit .277, which is all right if a player can field or hit home runs. But Rose showed little power and made a league-leading 36 errors at second base. Another problem was his size. Rose was still only 5 feet 9 and 155 pounds. When Harry Rose snuck a look at the Reds' internal scouting report on Pete's first season, he was crushed. It read: "He can't make a double play, can't throw, can't hit left-handed and can't run." The report did say that Rose showed a lot of hustle.

That was an understatement. Modeling himself on Enos "Country" Slaughter of the old St. Louis Cardinals, Rose hustled as much as anyone who ever played. He was always pushing for the extra base, stretching singles into doubles and doubles into triples. Like Slaughter, Rose always slid headfirst instead of feet first like everyone else. It was a technique that may not have gotten him to the base any sooner, but

Harry and Pete Rose in 1971, when Pete was a star with the Cincinnati Reds. Throughout his life, Pete had tried to model himself after his father, a man of strong principles who was also a legendary amateur athlete.

it excited the fans. As Rose liked to say, it got his picture in the paper.

Rose reacted to his poor season at Geneva by reporting to the Winter Instructional League in Florida, eager to improve his fielding. Even his fellow minor leaguers were impressed by Rose's single-mindedness. "It wasn't that Pete put in more time," said former Geneva teammate Art Shamsky, "but he practiced right. It was all work for him. The rest of us were *hoping* we'd make it. Pete was preparing."

After the end of the Instructional League season, Rose tried to add some bulk to his skinny frame by taking a job loading railroad boxcars in Cincinnati. The hours of heavy lifting and his mother's cooking did the trick. By the time he arrived for spring training with Class A Tampa in the Florida State League, Rose had grown 2 inches and gained 20 pounds of solid muscle.

In Tampa, all of Rose's hard work began to pay off. He fought second base to a draw, becoming adequate at turning the double-play pivot and making only 21 errors. And he hit .331, collecting a league-leading 160 hits in only 130 games. Former major league pitcher Johnny Vander Meer, who managed Tampa that year, built his offense around speed and line drives. That suited Rose just fine. "Every time I looked up," Vander Meer remembered, "he was driving one into the alleys and running like a scalded dog and sliding headfirst into third."

In 1962, the Reds promoted Rose to Macon in the South Atlantic (Sally) League, where they concentrated most of their top prospects. Rose finished the 1962 season with a .330 average. He led the Sally League in runs with 136 and triples with 17. He even hit 9 homers. He had won over the Macon fans with his all-out hustle, and more important for his career, he finally made believers in high places. During baseball's Winter Meetings of 1962–63, Reds manager Fred Hutchinson confided to a Cincinnati reporter that he was toying with the idea of promoting the cocky kid to the majors. "If I had any guts," Hutchinson said, "I'd stick Rose at second base and just forget about him."

4

CHARLIE HUSTLE

The Reds invited Pete Rose to their major league spring training camp in 1963. Not that there was a job for him to win. The team wanted Rose and a few of their other blue-chip prospects to get a taste of the big leagues to take with them back to the minors. Having never played a game above the A level, Rose was not a serious candidate for promotion to the Reds. The current Reds second baseman was a veteran named Don Blasingame. Blasingame, or "Blazer" as he was called, was a smooth fielder coming off a solid year with the bat. Besides, the team was not looking to make any changes in a lineup that had won 191 games over the previous two seasons. The Reds had gone to the World Series in 1961, had just missed winning the pennant in 1962, and were expected to contend again in 1963.

Rose did not care about all that. As he would later tell the story, "Second base wasn't up for grabs with Blazer there. But hell, I still wanted to grab for it." Rose was already a favorite of manager Fred Hutchinson's, and he was determined to play harder and hustle more than anyone in the Reds camp. He planned to make it as hard as possible for Hutchinson to send him back to the minors.

Rose demonstrates his batting stance for photographers at Chicago's Wrigley Field in September 1963. After finishing the season with a .273 batting average and 101 runs scored, Rose was voted the National League rookie of the year.

Rose hustled his way into the opening game of the preseason. He was not in the starting lineup, but he lingered in the Reds clubhouse after he and the rest of the minor leaguers had completed their morning workouts. Mike Ryba, a Reds minor league manager, saw him and said, "Hang around, Pete. Who knows? Hutch may need you as a pinch-runner or a pinch-hitter." The game went into extra innings, and sure enough, Rose was called upon to pinch-run. He stayed in the game at second base and later doubled twice. He scored the winning run in the 14th inning.

Rose went on to have a great spring, while Blasingame nursed a leg injury. Hutchinson began to think that the brash phenom was just what he needed to light a fire under some of the Reds' comfortable veterans. If an established player like Blasingame could lose his job to a rookie, then nobody's job was safe. That kind of insecurity, Hutchinson knew, has a way of making ballplayers play a little bit harder. Naturally, the team's veterans did not like the situation, and they blamed Rose. They gave him the cold shoulder and ridiculed his style of play. On one occasion, Rose's roommate locked him out of his hotel room in the middle of the night.

Veteran players on other teams took a dislike to Rose, too. One day, the Reds played an exhibition game against the New York Yankees. This was the great Yankees dynasty that was coming off an incredible run of 12 American League pennants in 14 seasons. The stars of that team, Mickey Mantle, Yogi Berra, and Whitey Ford, carried an aura that went beyond respect for their playing skills. The Yankees set the standard for how major league players dressed, how

Don Blasingame, known as "Blazer," was the Cincinnati second baseman when Rose came to spring training with the Reds in 1963. When Rose was unexpectedly chosen to replace the popular veteran in the starting lineup, the other Reds players showed their resentment by shunning the brash rookie.

they talked, and how they carried themselves on and off the field. And in their eyes, everything about Pete Rose, from his cockiness to his running out walks—even the fact that he did not drink—was wrong. It was Yankees pitching ace Whitey Ford who gave Rose his famous nickname. Watching the rookie during a 1963 exhibition game, Ford turned to Mantle and said in a mocking tone, "Hey, look at Charlie Hustle."

If Rose cared what the Yankees or anyone else thought about him, it did not show. He finished spring training on a hitting tear. The night before the Reds were scheduled to open the season at home against the Pittsburgh Pirates, Hutchinson called Rose into his office. "I've had them book you a hotel room," Hutchinson said. "I don't want you going home." When Rose asked why not, the manager replied, "I'm promoting you to the Reds. You're our starting second baseman. The word is going out and I don't want the neighbors bothering you all night." With that, Hutchinson handed Rose his first major league contract.

When Rose was introduced to a capacity crowd at Crosley Field on Opening Day, 1963, Harry Rose, LaVerne Rose, and the rest of the Reds fans gave him a loud standing ovation. Playing second base and batting second, he walked his first time up and then scored when Frank Robinson homered with two out in the first inning. The Reds won, 5–2. Five days later, Rose got his first major league hit. Appropriately enough, it was a double that he stretched into a triple with a wild headfirst slide.

Rose had achieved his childhood dream of playing for the Cincinnati Reds. But within a few weeks, the dream began to turn into a nightmare as he fell into a slump. When he reached 4 for 23, Hutchinson benched him and put

Rose shares a soft drink with future Hall of Famer Frank Robinson, one of the few Cincinnati veterans who befriended him during his rookie season. Robinson, the only man to win the Most Valuable Player Award in both leagues, also became the first black manager in baseball history.

Blasingame back at second. "Once the season began," the manager explained, "he was too overanxious. It was tough playing at home and he was on the spot." By early May, however, Rose bounced back. He had used his time on the bench to study National League pitchers, and soon he was back in his spring training groove. On July 1, with Rose banging out line drives left and right, the Reds sold Blasingame to the Washington Senators. Rose finished the 1963 season at .273, with 9 triples and 101 runs scored. In the off-season, the baseball writers voted him the National League rookie of the year by a wide margin.

Unfortunately, no matter how well he played, the hard feelings between Rose and some of the Reds veterans would not go away. Rejected by Blasingame's clique, which happened to be white, Rose was taken under the wing of future Hall of Famer Frank Robinson and other African-American players on the Reds.

"The only ones who treated me like a human being were the black players," Rose recalled, "guys like Frank Robinson and Vada Pinson. They gave me advice and treated me like a member of the team." The Reds front office blamed Rose for creating racial problems on the team. Team officials actually called him in and told him to stay away from Robinson because it was "bad for his image" to be seen in public with African-American players. To his credit, Rose ignored them. He could not see anything wrong with socializing with a man who had won an MVP Award. "They were great players I'd admired for years," Rose said. "I was flattered they made me feel a friend of theirs."

Rose makes the pivot on the front end of a double play during the 1965 All-Star Game. Though he began his career as a second baseman, the versatile Rose eventually played left field, center field, third base, and first base as well.

5

"I PLAY TO WIN"

The prime years for most ballplayers come between the ages of 25 and 29. Pete Rose turned 25 in 1966. As Rose entered the prime of his career, he and the Reds were going in opposite directions. The championship team of 1961 slowly fell apart. Fred Hutchinson died of cancer in 1964, and the following year the Reds shipped Frank Robinson to Baltimore in one of the most disastrous trades in baseball history. After winning 90 games three times in between 1961 and 1964, the team dropped to fourth place in 1965 and seventh in 1966.

Meanwhile, Rose's career flourished. He batted .300 for the first time in 1965. He made the All-Star team in 1965, 1967, 1968, and 1969. Even though he did not get much national exposure with his team going nowhere, Rose became unbelievably popular in the city of Cincinnati. When he was benched during a slump, the fans unfurled huge banners in protest. The Cincinnati press and fans ate up Rose's brash-kid style on and off the field. Asked in an interview why he ran down to first after a walk, Rose said, "There's no sense hanging around home plate when you could be on first."

Starting out with very few raw baseball tools, Rose made himself into a versatile, all-around player. He never seemed to stop running. One teammate explained, "It took a while to accept Pete, to see that he wasn't trying to show you up. He made you hustle because you were always afraid that he was going to run right over you if you didn't. . . . He even runs to the shower."

Some baseball skills are unteachable; no one can learn the strength to hit 40 home runs or the speed to steal 80 bases. But if someone made a list of all the baseball skills that can be learned and another list of all Pete Rose's strengths as a player, the two lists would be the same. By the late 1960s, Rose was a consistent .300 hitter, drew walks, and had good doubles and triples power. He hit 40 or more doubles seven times and had 11 triples three times. On pure smarts, he stole between 10 and 20 bases in 10 different seasons.

Above all, Rose was a leadoff hitter. It was his job to get on base, run the bases intelligently and aggressively, and score runs. In all these areas, Rose was one of the very best. He scored 100 or more runs in a season 10 times and led the National League in runs 4 times.

A lot of Rose's hard work in the early years went into making himself a decent major league second baseman. In 1967, Reds manager Dave Bristol decided to move him to left field to make room for glove man Tommy Helms. Instead of sulking, the 26-year-old Rose attacked his new position with the same energy and abandon he showed when breaking up a double play with a hard slide. "If I can make the All-Star team as an infielder," Rose vowed, "I can make it as an outfielder."

A year later, Rose just as cheerfully moved over to center field, and then to right field, in order to accommodate hard-hitting (and hard-fielding) Alex Johnson. In one game against the Atlanta Braves, Johnson ran to the wall and leaped to snare a long drive off the bat of Hank Aaron. The ball bounced off Johnson's hands and rebounded into the outstretched glove of Rose, who had hustled all the way over from center to back up the play. A few innings later, when Johnson muffed a line drive hit right at him, he turned toward Rose and asked, "Where the hell were you?"

In spite of having to learn to play three new positions in two years, Rose raised his game another notch at the plate, winning his first batting titles in 1968 and 1969 with averages of .335 and .348. Both titles came after close races that went down to the final day of the season.

The batting titles finally brought Rose his share of national recognition. However, what most baseball fans remember from this phase of his career is Rose's performance in the 1970 All-Star Game, which took place at Cincinnati's spanking new Riverfront Stadium.

Using his trademark headfirst slide, Rose beats the ball to third base in a 1966 game between the Reds and the Los Angeles Dodgers. Though the Reds fell out of contention during the mid-1960s, Rose's heroics kept the fans coming to the ballpark.

Facing Jim Palmer, Sam McDowell, and Jim Perry, the National League bats were quiet until the bottom of the ninth, when Dick Dietz's homer off Catfish Hunter sparked a three-run rally that tied the score at 4–4. That was how the score remained until the bottom of the 12th. Then, with two out, Rose singled sharply to center field off left-hander Clyde Wright of the Angels. Another single by Billy Grabarkewitz moved Rose up to second.

Rose knew that he represented the winning run. Since he did not have to worry about getting doubled off on a line drive with two outs, he took a big lead and reminded himself to sprint for third as soon as the batter, Jim Hickman, made contact. He was determined to score on any kind of base hit.

Hickman came through with a base hit to center field, and Rose was off and running. As he rounded third and headed for home, Rose saw Cleveland Indians catcher Ray Fosse move a few feet up the third-base line, blocking the plate as he set himself to catch the throw from center fielder Amos Otis.

Fosse was a promising 23-year-old who would finish the year with 18 home runs and a .307 batting average. He was also a casual friend of Rose's. Together with another couple, Fosse and his wife had had dinner at Rose's home the night before the game.

There was only a second or two for Rose to consider his options. If he tried to dance around Fosse, he would probably be tagged out. He thought about trying to slide headfirst. But, as Rose later recalled, "I knew that if I did I would get my head between his legs and break both collarbones." If he could not go around or under

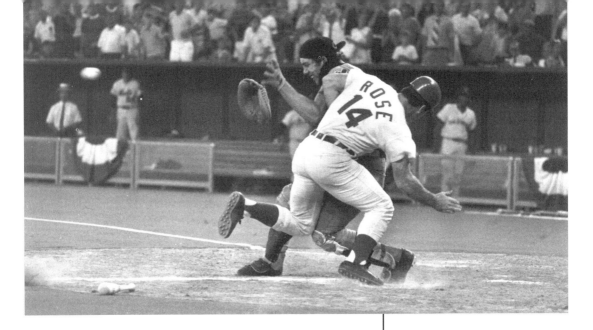

Fosse, then he would have to go through him. On the dead run Rose gathered his momentum, left his feet, and drove his shoulder into the catcher's midsection. Both men went sprawling on top of home plate as the ball went sailing past. Rose tagged the plate with his hand, and the National League won the game, 5–4.

The collision left Rose with an assortment of bruises that caused him to miss the next three games. Fosse suffered a separated shoulder that permanently ruined his throwing arm, his swing, and his chance of becoming a star. He played only two more seasons as a first-string catcher and retired in 1979.

There is no question that Rose's play was perfectly legal. A catcher knows that he risks being run into whenever he uses his body to block the plate. Fosse himself never complained, but some observers did wonder if it was really necessary for Rose to make such an aggressive play in a game that did not count in the standings. Interviewed after the All-Star Game, Rose gave his answer. "I play to win," he said. "Period."

Rose barrels into Cleveland Indians catcher Ray Fosse seconds before scoring the winning run in the 1970 All-Star Game, played in Cincinnati. Rose's tally gave the National League a 12th-inning, 5–4 victory.

THE BIG RED MACHINE

Pete Rose turned 31 in 1972. Though middle-aged by baseball standards, he still played with the hustle and joy of a rookie. Of course, he was no longer a boy. His father, Harry, had died suddenly of a heart attack in 1970. When Pete was breaking into professional baseball, he always said that he was playing for his father. Now he was on his own.

He was also a father himself: his daughter, Fawn, had been born in 1964, and his son, Pete junior, in 1969. Rose also played a paternal role for some of his teammates on the Cincinnati Reds of the 1970s. Remembering how rough the veterans had made it for him as a young player, Rose tried to show young players how to play and live like major leaguers. As former Reds second baseman Joe Morgan later recalled, "He was a guy who didn't drink or smoke, who went out of his way to be helpful to others, particularly young players. He used his familiarity with Cincinnati to help younger players find apartments, schools for their kids, the whole thing."

Rose was just as unselfish on the playing field. It is a cliché in baseball that players find it easy to pull together on winning teams, and there have been few teams in baseball history that did as much winning as the so-called Big Red Machine, which was put together by Reds general manager Bob Howsam and skillfully managed by Sparky Anderson. But playing for the Reds of the 1970s was sometimes hard on Rose's ego. For the first part of Rose's career, he had been Cincinnati's number one sports star. By the early 1970s, however, the Reds had developed future Hall of Fame catcher Johnny Bench, slugging first baseman Tony Perez, and shortstop Dave Concepcion. In a trade with Houston, the team had acquired Joe Morgan, one of the greatest second basemen of all time. On a list of the most talented Reds from that time, Rose would definitely follow Bench, Morgan, and Perez. It could be argued that Concepcion and outfielders Ken Griffey and George Foster were better players as well. "From 1968 till I got there in 1972," Morgan explained, "Pete's popularity had gone from the very heights to somewhere in mid-range. In 1972, he was no longer quite the star he once had been, and for sure it bothered him."

Rose did not let his ego get in the way of winning baseball games. He again changed defensive positions without complaint, going to left field in 1972 to make way for Cesar Geronimo, and going back to the infield in 1975, when he moved to third base so that George Foster could play left. Rose consistently sparked the Big Red Machine's offense from the leadoff slot. From 1972 to 1976, he scored 100 runs or more every year. He led the National League three times in runs scored, three times in hits, and three times in doubles. In 1973, Rose won his third batting

title with a .338 mark and was voted the National League's most valuable player. The Reds rolled with him, winning five division titles and four pennants between 1970 and 1976 and capturing the World Series in both 1975 and 1976.

As Rose accumulated 200-hit seasons, the decade was punctuated by a succession of important milestones. He got his 1,500th hit in 1970, his 2,000th in 1973, and his 2,500th in 1975. Reporters began to ask him about the magic 3,000 mark, considered an automatic ticket to the Baseball Hall of Fame in

Cincinnati's Johnny Bench, one of baseball's all-time greats, tags out an Oakland baserunner during the 1972 World Series. Led by Bench, Rose, and a host of other stars, Cincinnati's Big Red Machine won five division titles, four pennants, and two world championships between 1970 and 1976.

Rose looks on as second baseman Joe Morgan (center) and first baseman Tony Perez share a laugh during infield practice in 1975. Though he was no longer the Reds' number one player, Rose consistently hit .300 in the leadoff spot and played a solid third base.

Cooperstown, New York. "I really don't like to think about my 3,000th hit," Rose said. "Besides, when I get close to it, it'll mean my playing career will be nearing an end."

Rose underestimated his own durability. He got hit number 3,000 on May 5, 1978, at age 37. He celebrated by taking a run at one of baseball's most sacred records—Joe Di-Maggio's 56-game hitting streak, set in 1941. Rose's streak began on June 14. On July 31, Rose hit in his 44th straight game. He had now tied the National League record, set way back in 1897 by Wee Willie Keeler of the old National

League Baltimore Orioles. Rose lost his chance at DiMaggio the next day, when he struck out in his final at-bat on a 2-2 change-up by the Braves' Gene Garber; but he had electrified the sports world for a good part of the summer, and many fans who had previously resented his cockiness found themselves rooting for him.

The hitting streak turned out to be Rose's last hurrah as a Cincinnati Red. His contract with the team was up at the end of the 1978 season, and baseball's new system of free agency made it possible for players with six years in the majors to sell their services to the highest bidder. Rose wanted to stay in Cincinnati, but his feelings were hurt when he sensed that the Reds were not making a serious effort to upgrade his $365,000 salary to a figure that reflected his worth on the open market. He was also upset when the Reds fired his good friend Sparky Anderson during the off-season. Thus, when the Philadelphia Phillies offered to make Rose the highest-paid player in baseball at $3.2 million over four years, he said yes.

The Phillies were frustrated. They had won the National League East in 1976, 1977, and 1978, only to be beaten in the playoffs. They were hoping that Rose could put them over the hump and get them into their first World Series since 1950. He rose to the occasion, batting .331 and quickly mastering yet another new defensive position, first base. However, the rest of the team failed to follow his lead, and the Phillies finished a disappointing fourth in 1979.

Under new manager Dallas Green, the Phillies finally won their world championship in 1980. They would not have made it without Pete Rose. Even though he slipped to .282 during the

Stroking a single to the opposite field on July 25, 1978, Rose hits safely in his 38th consecutive game, setting a new National League record for 20th-century players. A week later, he ended his streak at 44 games, tying the all-time N.L. record set in 1897 by Wee Willie Keeler.

regular season, Rose exploded in the postseason. He batted .400 with three runs scored in the Phillies' dramatic playoff victory over Houston and Rose's old friend Joe Morgan.

In Game 6 of the 1980 World Series, Rose showed baseball fans why the Phillies had spent so much money to sign him. The Phillies were leading the Kansas City Royals, 3 games to 2, and they held a 4–1 lead going into the ninth inning. The Royals rallied, loading the bases with one out and the dangerous Frank White coming up. White hit a foul pop-up down the first-base line. Phillies catcher Bob Boone sprinted over to the edge of the dugout, held out his glove, and dropped the ball. But White never got another chance to hit. Rose had hustled over from first base to back up Boone. When he

saw the ball pop out of the catcher's mitt, he quickly reached down and snared it just inches from the ground. When Willie Wilson, the next Royals hitter, struck out, the Phillies became world champions.

After the peak of the World Series, Rose appeared to go downhill rapidly. He batted .325 in 1981, but with an alarming drop-off in power. In 1982 his average fell to .271, his lowest mark since he hit .269 as a green second-year man in 1964. In 1983, Rose's average dropped to .245; at the end of the season, the Phillies announced that they would not offer the 42-year-old superstar a new contract.

Most players in Rose's position would have seriously considered retirement. But in Rose's mind, he was no longer competing against the rest of the National League. He was competing for his place in the baseball record books. In August 1981, he had tied Stan Musial for the National League record for career hits at 3,630, and he began to set his sights on Ty Cobb's all-time major league mark of 4,191. "I can't do it this year," he reasoned in a 1981 interview, "I can't do it next year. But it's definitely something worth thinking about."

Rose ended the 1983 season with 3,990 hits, but his chances of catching Ty Cobb seemed very slim: he was in the free-agent market once again, and months went by without any team making him an offer. The 202 hits he needed might just as well have been 2,002.

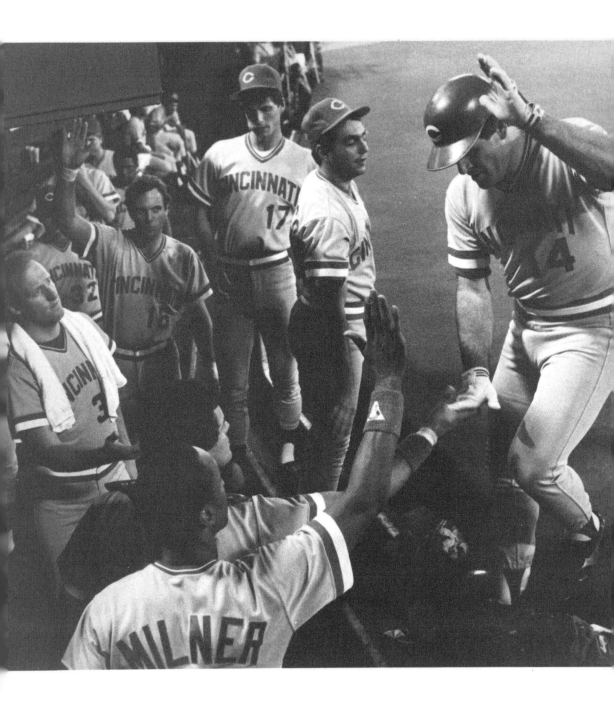

"I NEVER BET BASEBALL"

Many baseball people were surprised when the Montreal Expos signed Pete Rose to a contract for the 1984 season. Some suggested that Rose was washed up and that the Expos wanted him only as a publicity stunt. Rose himself bristled at the idea. "For those who think I can't play anymore," he said, "Montreal gave me a contract and they're a pretty good team. There's nothing I can do about the date I was born. I wish people would forget how damned old I am. I don't feel old, I don't act old and medical experts have told me my body isn't old."

Expos manager Bill Virdon must have been talking to those same experts, because when the 1984 season opened, Rose was Montreal's everyday left fielder. He rapped out five hits in the team's first series, and when the Expos arrived in Cincinnati to take on the Reds, he was only five hits away from the 4,000 mark. After opening the three-game series with a pair of two-hit games, Rose came into the game of April 11 needing only one more hit.

Rose drew four walks in the game and missed his chance to reach 4,000 hits in front of the Cincinnati fans. The milestone came two days later, on Friday the 13th, in the Expos' home

Rose is congratulated by teammates in September 1985, after delivering his 4,186th career hit, leaving him only 5 hits behind Ty Cobb. At this point in his pursuit of the all-time record, Rose was obsessed with Cobb; he even traded one of his World Series rings for a statue of the former Tigers star.

49

opener against the Phillies. The big hit, a double off Jerry Koosman, was greeted with a standing ovation from the Montreal fans. But there were few other highlights for Rose in Montreal. Nursing foot and arm injuries, he was hitting in the low .200s by mid-August and found himself riding the bench.

Reuven Katz, Rose's Cincinnati-based agent, began to talk with Reds general manager Bob Howsam about bringing Rose back to Cincinnati. The Expos then agreed to trade Rose for Reds infielder Tom Lawless. At first, the Reds wanted Rose only as a manager, but Rose and his agent insisted that he would only come home if he could continue his pursuit of Ty Cobb's record as a player-manager. The Reds agreed, and Rose returned to Cincinnati for a press conference on August 16. For his part, Rose took a pay cut of more than 50 percent.

To no one's surprise, Rose put his own name on the lineup card for the August 17 game against Chicago. Over 35,000 fans—the largest Riverfront Stadium crowd since opening day— came out to welcome Rose back to Cincinnati. None of them went home disappointed. Rose drove in a run with a single in the first inning and then raced to third base on a throwing error. On the play, he delighted the crowd with a headfirst slide that kicked up a cloud of dust. Charlie Hustle was back.

In 1985, Rose's first full year as manager, the Reds improved from 70-92 and fifth place to 89-72 and second place, 5½ games behind the Los Angeles Dodgers. Cincinnati might have finished even closer to the top if Rose had not insisted on giving 400 at-bats to a 44-year-old first baseman who hit .264 with no power, but most Reds fans did not mind. Like the rest of the country, the Cincinnati fans were completely wrapped up in Rose's final assault on Ty Cobb's record, which ended triumphantly on September 11.

Rose's last at-bat came on August 17, 1986, when he struck out swinging against San Diego Padres reliever Goose Gossage. But Rose never officially announced his retirement. He seemed to have trouble accepting that his 24-year career had finally come to an end.

Certainly, there were no more records left for Rose to shoot for. He had 4,256 hits, more than anyone else in baseball history, and the rest of his records would fill a book. Among them are the record for most games, lifetime, 3,562; most singles, lifetime, 3,215; most seasons with 100 or more games played, 23; most seasons with 200 or more hits, 10; most seasons 150 or more games played, 17; most at-bats lifetime, 14,053; and most seasons with 600 or more at-bats, 17.

With numbers like these, Rose should have been a shoo-in for the Hall of Fame. Many people expected the baseball writers to elect him unanimously in his first year of eligibility, which was to come in 1991.

But as of 1994, Rose was still waiting for his first Hall of Fame vote. In 1989, Rose had agreed to be placed on baseball's "permanently ineligible" list. People in this category are banned from major league baseball for life, and they are not eligible to be considered for election to the Hall of Fame. The events leading up to this shocking development began in February, when Baseball Commissioner Peter Ueberroth called Rose to his New York City office to answer charges that he was involved with illegal book-

Judge Kenesaw Mountain Landis was appointed baseball's first commissioner in 1920, after eight members of the Chicago White Sox were indicted for plotting to throw the 1919 World Series. Though the players were acquitted by a Chicago jury, Landis banned them all from baseball for life.

makers and that he had placed bets on baseball games.

Baseball officials take the issue of gambling very seriously. In 1919, eight members of the Chicago White Sox took money from gamblers to throw the World Series to the Cincinnati Reds. When the scandal broke, club owners feared that the game would be totally discredited in the eyes of the public unless they acted decisively. The owners appointed Judge Kenesaw Mountain Landis as the game's first commissioner, and Landis promptly banned the eight "Black Sox" from baseball for life. One of them, the great Shoeless Joe Jackson, has never been on the ballot for the Hall of Fame despite his .356 lifetime batting average, the third highest in history.

Since 1919, baseball has been almost paranoid about gambling. In 1944, Landis kicked Philadelphia Phillies owner William Cox out of baseball for betting on his own team *to win.* In

1947, Landis's successor, Happy Chandler, suspended Dodgers manager Leo Durocher for one season. Durocher had not placed any bets, but he had associated with gamblers and mobsters, and that was enough. Because of cases like these, everybody in baseball knows the rules. Anyone who gets involved with gamblers or shady characters is risking suspension. Anyone who bets on baseball games will certainly be banned for life.

The rumors that led to Ueberroth's questioning of Rose came from Paul Janszen, a dealer in illegal steroids who had worked as a government informant in a drug case. Janszen claimed to federal agents that he was a close friend of Rose's and that he knew a lot about Rose and illegal gambling. When Rose met with Ueberroth, he told the commissioner that he had not bet on baseball and that he did not owe money to illegal bookmakers. "There was nothing ominous," Ueberroth told the newspapers after the meeting, "and there will be no follow through." But a few days later, Ueberroth hired former federal prosecutor John Dowd to conduct a formal investigation into the charges.

By May 1989, when Dowd turned in a 225-page report on his investigation, Ueberroth had been replaced as commissioner by A. Bartlett Giamatti. Dowd's report attempted to build a case that Rose had associated with shady characters; that he had bet large sums of money with illegal bookmakers on a variety of sports; and finally, that he had also bet on his own team, the Reds. The report contained plenty of evidence to back up the first two charges. But it was far less convincing on the question of whether Rose had committed the cardinal sin of betting on baseball. Virtually all of the evidence on that point came from the testimony of convicted criminal Paul Janszen; an illegal bookmaker named Ron Peters, who had taken bets from Janszen; and two of Janszen's friends.

As details of the report began to leak out, friends and ex-teammates of Rose's expressed disbelief that he would bet on baseball. They knew that Rose liked to gamble; he had gambled on horses, dogs, and sports other than baseball for most of his adult life. Some people even thought Rose's gambling was out of control. More than once during his career, friends or front-office officials had spoken to Rose about his gambling or his choice of associates. But for Rose to bet on baseball was unthinkable.

For his part, Rose completely denied betting on baseball. He accused Janszen of attempting to frame him. Janszen's motive, according to Rose, was revenge for being dropped as a friend when Rose found out that he was involved with drug dealing. Rose also claimed that Janszen had once tried to extort money from him and threatened blackmail if Rose refused to pay. "He said he was going to tell the Commissioner I bet on baseball," Rose said.

Normally, the next step would have been for Commissioner Giamatti to hold a hearing on the charges and get Rose's side of the story. But this never happened. In June, Rose and his lawyers went to the Cincinnati court of Judge Norbert Nadel to stop Giamatti from holding the hearing. They argued that Giamatti should not be allowed to preside over the hearing because of a letter he had written to another judge, Carl Rubin, who was about to sentence Ron Peters on drug and tax charges. In his letter to the judge, Giamatti stated that he had found Peters's testimony to Dowd to be truthful. If the commissioner had already decided that he believed one of Rose's main accusers, how could he conduct a fair and impartial hearing?

Judge Nadel thought that was a good question, and he ordered baseball not to proceed with the Rose case. The Nadel decision was followed by two months of legal wrangling between Rose and the commissioner's office. Meanwhile, Rose learned that he was being investigated by a federal grand jury for tax evasion.

On August 23, Rose and Giamatti agreed to the settlement. Rose accepted lifetime banishment, and Giamatti agreed that he would make no formal finding that Rose had bet on baseball. The settlement satisfied Giamatti because it removed the danger that the courts might use his ill-considered letter to prevent baseball from ever disciplining Rose. This would be embarrassing both to baseball and to Giamatti personally.

Rose's motives in agreeing to such a harsh penalty are less obvious. The pending tax eva-

At an August 24, 1989, news conference, Baseball Commissioner A. Bartlett Giamatti announces that Pete Rose has agreed to be placed on baseball's "permanently ineligible" list.

sion charges may have been his primary reason. The grand jury was looking into evidence that Rose had not paid taxes on income from card shows, the sale of memorabilia, and gambling. Any hearing by the baseball commissioner into Rose's gambling activities could have turned up damaging evidence that prosecutors could use in the tax case. Ultimately, Rose pleaded guilty to evading taxes anyway. In 1990, he paid his back taxes and a $50,000 fine. He served five months in prison, and after his release he performed 1,000 hours of community service.

In addition, Rose may have felt that the settlement at least gave him a chance of eventually going into the Hall of Fame: if the commissioner had officially ruled that Rose had bet on baseball, his election would have been out of the question. Baseball's rules allow players on the permanently ineligible list to apply for reinstatement on a yearly basis. Rose apparently got the impression during his meeting with Giamatti that the commissioner was willing to reinstate him at some point in the future.

On the day the settlement with Giamatti was announced, Rose spoke to the press in Cincinnati. He was defiant and almost cheerful. He refused to back off one inch from his claim that he had never bet on baseball: "Obviously I've made some mistakes," he said, "but one of the mistakes wasn't betting on baseball."

Rose's mood changed quickly when he heard what Bart Giamatti had to say in his own press conference in New York. Giamatti explained that he had made no official finding that Rose had bet on baseball. Then a reporter asked him what his personal opinion was. Incredibly, Giamatti said that he believed that Rose had bet on baseball.

Rose felt that he had been double-crossed: "I was dumbfounded that he would say that. Just twelve hours earlier we signed that agreement in good faith, and there he was saying he thought I bet on baseball. The only reason I signed that agreement was that it had no finding that I bet on baseball." Later Rose added, "In some other life, I'm going to talk to [Giamatti] about that."

Bart Giamatti died of a heart attack a few days after that press conference. Today, Rose lives in a kind of baseball purgatory. He remains on the permanently ineligible list and cannot appear on a Hall of Fame ballot. He cannot hold a job in major league baseball or even walk into a major league clubhouse to visit with old friends. Pete Rose has admitted to a lot of mistakes, including cheating on his taxes, gambling too much, and being "a lousy chooser of friends." But Rose still maintains that he was framed by Janszen and Peters and betrayed by Giamatti. "I never bet baseball," he said recently, "I swear I never bet baseball."

Surrounded by reporters, a somber Rose makes his way into Cincinnati's federal courthouse in July 1990. After serving a brief prison term for tax evasion, Rose embarked on a number of successful business ventures—but he remained an outcast from the game he had played with such passion.

CHRONOLOGY

1941	Born Peter Edward Rose in Cincinnati, Ohio, on April 14
1960	Signs professional baseball contract with Cincinnati Reds; begins career with Geneva, New York, at lowest level of minor leagues
1962	Promoted to Macon in the South Atlantic (Sally) League
1963	Rose wins second base job with the Reds in spring training; makes his major league debut on opening day; wins Rookie of the Year Award after batting .271
1965	Makes All-Star team for the first time
1967	Reds manager Dave Bristol shifts Rose's position from second base to left field
1968–69	Rose wins his first batting titles, averaging .335 and .348 respectively, bringing national attention
1970	Scores winning run in the All-Star Game by running over catcher Ray Fosse; Fosse suffers separated shoulder that ruins his baseball career
1972–76	Rose scores 100 runs or more each year and leads National League three times in runs, hits, and doubles
1973	Wins his third batting title with .338 average, earning him the National League's Most Valuable Player Award
1975–76	Cincinnati's Big Red Machine wins the World Series two years in a row
1978	Rose gets his 3,000th hit; signs with Philadelphia Phillies as a free agent during the off-season
1980	Assists the Phillies in winning the World Series, after batting .400 in the playoffs
1981	Ties Stan Musial's National League record for career hits with 3,630
1984	Signs with Montreal Expos; is traded back to the Reds as player-manager
1985	Breaks Ty Cobb's record for all-time career hits (4,191) on·September 11, at Riverfront Stadium
1986	Has last at-bat on August 17; ends playing career with 4,256 hits, more than any player in baseball history
1989	Baseball commissioner's office investigates Rose's alleged gambling activities; Rose is placed on the "permanently ineligible" list as part of settlement that exonerates him from charge that he bet on baseball
1990	Convicted of tax evasion and serves five months in prison; remains ineligible for the Hall of Fame due to settlement with commissioner's office

MAJOR LEAGUE STATISTICS

CINCINNATI REDS, PHILADELPHIA PHILLIES, MONTREAL EXPOS

YEAR	TEAM	G	AB	R	H	2B	3B	HR	RBI	BA	SB
1963	CIN N	157	623	101	170	25	9	6	41	.273	13
1964		136	516	64	139	13	2	4	34	.269	4
1965		162	670	117	209	35	11	11	81	.312	8
1966		156	654	97	205	38	5	16	70	.313	4
1967		148	585	86	176	32	8	12	76	.301	11
1968		149	626	94	210	42	6	10	49	.335	3
1969		156	627	120	218	33	11	16	82	.348	7
1970		159	649	120	205	37	9	15	52	.316	12
1971		160	632	86	192	27	4	13	44	.304	13
1972		154	645	107	198	31	11	6	57	.307	10
1973		160	680	115	230	36	8	5	64	.338	10
1974		163	652	110	185	45	7	3	51	.284	2
1975		162	662	112	210	47	4	7	74	.317	0
1976		162	665	130	215	42	6	10	63	.323	9
1977		162	655	95	204	38	7	9	64	.311	16
1978		159	655	103	198	51	3	7	52	.302	13
1979	PHI N	163	628	90	208	40	5	4	59	.331	20
1980		162	655	95	185	42	1	1	64	.282	12
1981		107	431	73	140	18	5	0	33	.325	4
1982		162	634	80	172	25	4	3	54	.271	8
1983		151	493	52	121	14	3	0	45	.245	7
1984		121	374	43	107	15	2	0	34	.286	1
	2 Teams	MON N	(95G– .259)		CIN N (26G–.365)						
1985	CIN N	119	405	60	107	12	2	2	46	.264	8
1986		72	237	15	52	8	2	0	25	.219	3
Totals		3562	14053	2165	4256	746	135	160	1314	.303	198
World Series											
6 years		34	130	12	35	5	1	2	9	.269	1

FURTHER READING

Callahan, Tom. "The Sad Ordeal of Mr. Baseball." *Time,* April 3, 1989.

Drury, Bob. "Pete Rose, Manager." *Sport,* June 1985.

Goodman, Mark S. "Pete Rose Longs to Rise Again." *People Weekly,* September 2, 1991.

Okrent, Daniel. "Hardball." *The New York Times Book Review,* July 7, 1991.

Reilly, Rick. "A Rose Is a Rose." *Sports Illustrated,* August 16, 1993.

Reston, James, Jr. *Collision at Home Plate: The Lives of Pete Rose and Bart Giamatti.* New York: Burlingame Books, 1991.

Rose, Pete, and Hal Bodley. *Countdown to Cobb: My Diary of the Record-Breaking 1985 Season.* St. Louis: The Sporting News, 1985.

Rose, Pete, and Roger Kahn. *Pete Rose: My Story.* New York: Macmillan, 1989.

Rose, Pete, and Hal McCoy. *The Official Pete Rose Scrapbook.* New York: New American Library, 1985.

Sokolove, Michael Y. *Hustle: The Myth, Life, and Lies of Pete Rose.* New York: Simon & Schuster, 1990.

United Press International. *4192!: A Celebration of Pete Rose, Baseball's Record-Breaking Hitter.* Chicago: Contemporary Books, 1985.

INDEX

RE CREDITS
Wide World Photos: p. 57; the Cincinnati Historical Society: pp. 14, 18, 20, 23, 60; National Baseball Library,
erstown, NY: pp. 10, 31, 52; UPI/Bettmann: pp. 2, 8, 12, 25, 28, 32, 34–35, 37, 39, 40, 43, 44, 46, 48, 55, 58.

THOMAS W. GILBERT holds a degree in classics from Yale University. A former dictionary and textbook editor, he is the principal author of *150 Years of Baseball*, a history of the national pastime from its early days to the present. A frequent contributor to many national publications, Gilbert has also written *Roberto Clemente* in the Chelsea House HISPANICS OF ACHIEVEMENT series and is the author of the forthcoming volume *Baseball and the Color Line*.

JIM MURRAY, veteran sports columnist of the *Los Angeles Times*, is one of America's most acclaimed writers. He has been named "America's Best Sportswriter" by the National Association of Sportscasters and Sportswriters 14 times, was awarded the Red Smith Award, and was twice winner of the National Headliner Award. In addition, he was awarded the J. G. Taylor Spink Award in 1987 for "meritorious contributions to baseball writing." With this award came his 1988 induction into the National Baseball Hall of Fame in Cooperstown, New York. In 1990, Jim Murray was awarded the Pulitzer Prize for Commentary.

EARL WEAVER is the winningest manager in the Baltimore Orioles' history by a wide margin. He compiled 1,480 victories in his 17 years at the helm. After managing eight different minor league teams, he was given the chance to lead the Orioles in 1968. Under his leadership the Orioles finished lower than second place in the American League East only four times in 17 years. One of only 12 managers in big league history to have managed in four or more World Series, Earl was named Manager of the Year in 1979. The popular Weaver had his number 5 retired in 1982, joining Brooks Robinson, Frank Robinson, and Jim Palmer, whose numbers were retired previously. Earl Weaver continues his association with the professional baseball scene by writing, broadcasting, and coaching.